100 Business Girls Essentials

presents

70 Tips for Women in Business

A Compilation to Get Unstuck!

Jamillah Y. Johnson

To those seeking greatness, start where you are!

Copyright ©2015 by Jamillah Yaasmin Johnson

All rights reserved. This book, or parts thereof, may not be reproduced in any form without permission from the publisher; exceptions are made for brief excerpts used in published reviews. For more information email literarycandy@gmail.com.

Published by Literary Candy Books.

www.literarycandybooks.com

Second Edition.

Introduction

I was forced into entrepreneurship. It was a goal I always had, but I wasn't ready when it happened.

Upon receiving my Bachelor of Science in Sports and Recreation Management, I was unable to get a job. Not even an interview. Let me rephrase that, I did eventually land a "seasonal job" but was let go two months later.

You're probably thinking that I didn't have enough experience. Well you would be wrong. I had internships, volunteer experiences, and several years of employment under my belt, but I had to learn that sometimes it's just not meant to be. One of the many things that have changed in the last decade is that employers take more chances on young female employees. I have encountered age, sex, and racial discrimination to be quite honest.

If you want to do things you love, you can't wait for anyone. You have to go for it. Yes you will fail. I repeat, yes you will fail. Yes you will be broke. But if you're unemployed, you're broke anyway so why not spend time pursuing something you're passionate about and could potentially generate income?

While I was still in college, I created several successful membership based online forums though Yahoo! centered on entertainment, gossip, and sports. I partnered with a friend and started an entertainment newsletter called, The Streets and eventually it became one of the first online magazines.

Life is about trying out new things. Sometimes things can be ahead of their time as was the case with The Streets Online and the earlier versions of blogging.

In 2005, I became a full-time caretaker for my father, who had to have his lower leg amputated due to complications with diabetes. He was later diagnosed with kidney failure. A year later I had my daughter and it triggered a desire in me to go full steam ahead in becoming a consultant. I started Industry Consulting Group at first, where I offered business writing and marketing consulting. Eventually that became one with Signature Style Promotions, where I added public relations, event planning, and product placement services. I landed all of my first clients through connections on Myspace. True Story!

I learned many important lessons during this stage. For one, most of your hard work won't pay off because most of the people won't pay you. So always get a deposit upfront. Second, if the person you're working for isn't ready for the next level, your suggestions will fall on deaf ears. Third, startup entrepreneurs have a tendency to believe you will steal their ideas, so their extra protective and don't really want to offer up information that you need to help them. That's why confidentiality agreements exist.

Don't think starting your business will be a walk in the park. It's a constant work in progress and its work you have to be willing to do. There are obstacles you will face and trust me, you will get through them. You have to know when to throw in the towel as well as when it's time to step your game up.

Seeing and meeting a need is vital to the success of your business. I had the idea for #100BusinessGirls, because I felt with the influx of social media outlets, while they allowed us to add people, we weren't truly connecting and my longtime friend, Etophia Lane agreed. Nothing beats a face to face introduction and a great conversation.

In 2011, we hosted our first *Let's Do Brunch!* meetup and have been going strong ever since. The topics that are discussed in this book are from these events. I decided to compile all of the tips together to be a quick resource guide for women to always have as a reference. Whether you're an entrepreneur or not, the tips offered in this book are easy to follow.

#100Businessgirls is currently based in Philadelphia and New York City. We've also hosted events in Washington DC and Sag Harbor, New York. We aspire to host gatherings in other U.S. cities and internationally as well.

You are encouraged to share the topics discussed in this book with your networking groups. If you would like to connect with us, please visit www.100BusinessGirls.com and I can be reached personally by email at jamillah@100BusinessGirls.com. Feel free to share your suggestions and feedback on any of the topics that are discussed.

Enjoy the journey,

Jamillah

Branding Yourself & Your Business Online

Your brand is what people say about you when you're not in the room"

- Jeff Bezos, Founder of Amazon

Questions for You:

How do you brand yourself and your business online?

Are you concerned about your online reputation?

Tips:

1. Remember that your username is your identity. Select a name that is simple, memorable, and marketable. (Your name shouldn't be pussycat305, unless your company name is Pussy Cat Entertainment and it's based in Miami, Florida.)

2. Learn who's talking about you or your company. You can easily conduct a Google or Twitter search on this. Engage them in conversation, send an email introducing yourself, or thanking them for mentions. This is a great way to start building a relationship.

3. Find other professionals in your field, or closely related fields, on social networks. You want to set your profile up so that only people who you are interested in connecting with will come up in your list of suggestions.

4. Connect with old friend and business colleagues.

5. Discover new people through reading and learning, and follow the media they make on various social networks.

6. Learn about your competition through the media they make, and discover where you build or add value.

7. Manage elements of your online presence around your primary blog or website.

8. Use sites such as LinkedIn, Magnt.com, or About.me as your professional online portals. You want people to be able to search for you and find examples of your work.

9. To avoid unwanted drama, create online profiles that portray you in a professional light. If you must, create a personal page for friends and family and set that to private. And have a company page that is open to the public.

10. Be consistent and engage with your audience. You want to respond to inquiries within 48 hours anything beyond that should have an apology attached for your delayed response time.

Definition of a Business Woman

"Bravery is needed to have contrary opinions and to take unexpected paths. If you're not courageous, you're going to be hanging around the water cooler, talking about the guy who actually is."

Jessica Hagy

Questions for You:

How are you defining your business?

What challenges have you faced as a woman in business?

Tips:

1. Think Strategically - Look at something from more than one point of view.

2. Be Fearless - Don't let the fear of failure prevent you from taking risks. Fear will always be there. Do it anyway.

3. Don't let distractions throw you off course - Keep your eyes on the prize.

4. Personal Branding - Don't be afraid to reinvent yourself. Have more than one stream of income.

5. Communicate - Say what you mean & mean what you say. The clearest most productive and effective way to communicate is honestly and openly.

6. Initiate - Act without being told.

7. Always open yourself to meeting new people, new experiences, and collaborations that fall in line with your goals.

8. Share your knowledge & Learn from others.

Knowing and Loving Your Business: Being Prepared for the Next Level

"A genuine leader is not a searcher for consensus but a molder of consensus."

Dr. Martin Luther King, Jr.

Questions for you:

Have you ever been unprepared?

How did that work out for you?

What did you learn from that experience?

Tips:

1. Always Be Prepared

Be prepared to improvise. Have a plan B and C lined up and always do your best. Don't give up without trying.

2. Become the strategist your business needs

Sometimes we can't always afford to outsource. Spend time researching and learning new technology and techniques that will help your business and your knowledge base grow.

3. Know when it's time to ask for help

We can't do everything ourselves. Know when its time to seek interns to handle the major little things. If you are in need of a professional, ask someone you know experienced in an area you need assistance in and barter your services in exchange for their help. Collaborations are a brilliant way to help someone else while helping yourself.

4. Know Your Numbers

If you're seeking out investors, know the value of your business. If you offer products or services, never sell yourself short. Love your business enough to know it *NEEDS* money in order for it thrive. Place the oxygen mask over your face first.

5. Know when it's time for a break

Always take some time out to relax, relate, release, and refresh. Whether it's a weekend, a day, or 30 minutes. Take some time out to recharge your creative juices.

Questions for you (Part 2):

1. What is the next level for your business?

2. What do you need to get there?

Networking without Borders

"Pulling a good network together takes effort, sincerity and time."

- Alan Collins, author of "Unwritten HR Rules"

Questions for you:

Are you tapped into networks outside of your city?

How has it been beneficial for your personal and professional growth?

Tips:

1. Step Outside Your Comfort Zone – It takes guts to start a business, but don't just stop there. In order for your business to grow you must constantly meet new people. Everyone in your network has a network, so don't be afraid to turn to them for help.

2. Be Curious – Curiousity is the spark that fuels creativity. Research trends in other cities and countries besides your own. You might find something to apply to your business that could bring in alternative revenue.

3. Expand your relationships outside of your culture to increase your chances of meeting people who can assist you in expanding nationally, internationally.

4. Use online networking sites to connect with decision makers and key influencers.

5. Build A Cluster – Rather than view a similar business as competition, look to them as collaborative partners and create a support network.

The Power of Patience

"Patience and time do more than strength or passion."

Jean de La Fontaine

"Patience is passion tamed."

Lymon Abbott

Question for you:

As an entrepreneur, how have you exhibited patience in starting and/or operating your business?

Tips:

Patience is a key component of the recipe for business success. Although it is often a characteristic, it is also a skill that can be learned. People often start their businesses and expect immediate return on investment. It is important to remember that most businesses very often do not automatically yield profit. They actually go through a period of gestation where very little happens. If you do not have the patience to see your business through, it will ultimately fail.

By **HAVING PATIENCE** you:

- Become meticulous and attentive to important details.

- Think logically and use more common sense.

- More likely to be prepared and have goals in place.

- Understand your strengths and weaknesses.

- Will be able to establish your resources and needs and know how to manage them.

IMPATIENT people are:

    Much more impulsive.

    More likely to jump to conclusions.

    Make hasty decisions that ultimately cost their business.

THINGS TO REMEMBER:

    Have a healthy dose of **AMBITION** to establish your goals.

    Take the necessary steps towards those goals and evaluate along the way. Some will yield success and some may go horribly wrong and that is okay.

    Take action! Don't get stuck and never give up. You can always come back to a goal if it wasn't accomplished. Having patience will help you take those steps.

Who Does She Think She Is?

"If you are committed to creating value and if you aren't afraid of hard times, obstacles become utterly unimportant. A nuisance perhaps, but with no real power. The world respects creation; people will get out of your way."

Candice Carpenter, founder of iVillage.com

Questions for You:

How are you representing yourself as a woman in business?

Do you find that women are more or less likely to share their resources?

Tips:

1. **Keep a Positive Mind**
   Master the art of positive thinking. You are worthy and deserving of the best life has to offer, but you are also worthy and deserving of life's challenges.

2. **Accept Change**
   Change is a given. Everything must come to an end in order to allow growth.

3. **Consider yourself a VIP/Think & Act Like A CEO**
   Whether just starting your business, or working for others, always hold your head high.

4. **Control and Learn from Your Emotions**
   Always take a step back before reacting to a situation.

5. **Never Stop Learning**
   Don't get left behind. Stay up on current trends in your industry. Try being ahead of the curve.

6. **Know Your Value**
   Never sell yourself or your time short.

7. **Surround Yourself with Good People**
   Have a circle of people who encourage and support your ambition and can lend a helping hand if needed. Pay it forward.

8. Step Outside Your Comfort Zone
   Don't be afraid to try something new.

9. Celebrate Your Success
   Give yourself a pat on the back for a job well done. Do something you enjoy.

10. Celebrate Other's Success
    Congratulate your colleagues. Cheer for their success as if it were your own. Read about other's who are where you want to be and learn from them.

Social Networking:

Balancing Your Business & Personal Life Online

Too many people overvalue what they are not and undervalue what they are."

- Malcolm Forbes, Publisher

The days of hiding behind an online screen name and cute avatar are over. Now more than ever, people look to social media to find information about an individual or company.

Questions for You:

What does your online presence say about you?

How do you manage your online presence?

Tips:

1. Use Discernment – certain personal views shouldn't be shared online with the world and could have an impact on your professional life.

2. Something as simple as a profile photo can impact your brand, use photos that showcase you at your best.

3. Your personal social media accounts can be spontaneous, but you should have a strategic plan for what is posted on your business accounts.

4. Keep your friends and family aware of your business, but don't beat them over the head with it.

5. Consistency is Key -- Your brand personality says a lot about you. Make sure you keep your tone, word choices, and response time consistent with your audience.

6. Do an audit of your network. Learn who the people are that are following you because this is your core audience.

7. Everyone doesn't belong in your network. Ignore, Deny, Unfollow, Block, and repeat

when necessary. Especially if an individual may pose a problem to your reputation.

8. Don't engage in negative conversation about competitors or leaders in your industry online. If you need to vent, speak with a close friend in confidence.

9. Balance your self-promotion by promoting and helping others. This will make your followers more receptive to your promotional posts and more likely that they will pass it along.

10. If you ever get in the position that you feel the need to defend a negative comment or criticism, don't react right away. Take enough time to remove the venom from your thoughts before responding, if at all. Remember silence is golden and the online trolls will starve.

The Off Season Networking Advantage

How to Relax & Still Grow Your Business

This topic was originally entitled The Summertime Networking Advantage, but it was reworked to not only apply to the summer months but also to that time between Thanksgiving and New Year's Eve.

Questions for you:

Do you take advantage of attending holiday parties of local organizations?

Have you ever thought about hosting your own holiday or summer events? Even with your own personal contacts, you never know who knows who. (Think six degrees of separation.)

During the summer months and winter holidays, we tend to wind down our networking efforts. We suggest you throw that mindset down the drain, because these are opportune times to actually participate in fellowship with colleagues. Why? Because there are plenty of parties and people tend to be in better spirits. This is a great time to add to your network, meet potential clients, and connect with past ones.

Here are ways to engage:

Host a happy hour get together (This works well in summer or winter).

Host a sit down meal. (Weekend brunch is my personal favorite).

Send out holiday greetings via mail or email (Keep it generic to save time and money if you're printing cards).

Tips:

1. Take advantage of people's lighter schedules. Invite them out to coffee or lunch.

2. Improve your digital networking. Connect with people on social media and update your profiles.

3. Never leave home without your business cards. You never know who you might meet at a summertime get together.

4. Build/refresh your website – People will Google before they connect with you, so always keep your website updated with current news.

5. Access Goals – By now you should know if you're on track to reaching any goals you set in the beginning of the year. Go over any lists you made to make sure you're sticking to your plans. If not set up time to work on them.

6. Automate Your Business – Remember to set up email to respond while you're away.

7. Relax and take time for yourself -- As entrepreneurs we get accustomed to working non-stop, but this is your company always remember to give yourself some vacation time.

Winning with Integrity

"When you are content to be simply yourself and don't compare or compete, everyone will respect you."

Lao Tzu, *Tao Te Ching*

Questions for you:

Have you ever compromised your integrity?

How did you feel about the outcome?

"Living with integrity means: Not settling for less than what you know you deserve in your relationships; Asking for what you want and need from others; Speaking your truth, even though it might create conflict or tension; Behaving in ways that are in harmony with your personal values; Making choices based on what you believe, and not what others believe."

Barbara De Angelis, Best Selling Author

Tips:

1. Always treat others with professional respect and courtesy.

2. Honor your commitments and obligations. People want to do business with those they trust. Make sure you are a person of your word. Keep your appointments, show up on time, complete your projects, and most of all communicate with your clients.

3. Make sure your clients communicate with you and hold them accountable for their actions.

4. Don't let friends, family, or clients jeopardize the reputation of your business. Monitor your social media mentions, sometimes your personal circle doesn't factor in your branding when posting personal messages, invites or uploading photos tagging you in them.

5. Re-evaluate how your image and business are represented. Check your own marketing materials, website, blogs, social media, and evaluate how yourself and your business is being covered by others online.

6. Remain involved in community-related issues that fall in line with your beliefs. You want to be seen as a community contributor and you

want to stay involved, so choose something you are really passionate about.

7. Don't be afraid to walk away. As entrepreneurs, a lot of our business is dependent on others and if we're delivering the goods on time, we need to be paid for services – on time. Have all of your agreements in writing prior to starting any work. Never be afraid to drop clients who are disrespectful, high maintenance, or contract violators, etc. But before you end on bad terms, please refer back to tip #2 and #3.

Measuring Your Success

"Success is to be measured not so much by the position that one has reached in life as by the obstacles which he has overcome."

Booker T. Washington

Questions for You:

As an entrepreneur or professional, how do you measure your success?

What factors do you feel have propelled your success?

What factors do you feel have deterred your success?

Tips:

1. Set resolutions throughout the year, not just for the New Year.

2. If you slack off, there's nothing wrong with picking up where you left off or starting over. What's important is that you keep moving forward.

3. Record your goals in a notebook so that you are able to map everything out as you see it in your head. Nothing is too far-fetched when putting this exercise into practice. You might not be able to accomplish a goal by next week or month, but it doesn't mean it won't ever be possible.

4. Be patient.

5. Create a list of short and long term goals. Things that can be accomplished sooner should get first priority. Research counts as working towards your goals.

6. Always do your research before pursuing a new venture. There's a chance your new idea is already in existence, but don't let that discourage you. It means that you have a good idea. It just needs to have your signature on it.

7. Take time out to examine your progress to appreciate how far you have come.

8. Measure YOUR success against YOUR OWN success. With social media we are in constant contact with what our peers are doing and it can become competitive whether we realize it or not. Take what you see online with a grain of salt.

Bonus Tips

ReDefining a Woman's Worth

"Your Crown has been bought and paid for. All you must do is put it on."

James Baldwin

Questions for You:

Do you let the way you feel about yourself impact the way you handle your business?

How have you gone about finding a balance between your business and personal life while pursuing your dreams?

Tips:

1. **Self worth vs. Net worth** – When it comes to our net worth, most of us feel that we never quite measure up. We lower our financial and self value to appease others (make or keep friends, clients, etc). This has to stop. Your business and your bills can not sustain on this logic.

2. **Be okay with being paid well** – If you settle or expect less, you not only leave your potential on the table, but you leave a lot of money on the table as well.

3. **Seek to become someone you admire** – You are here to be your most valuable self and to express your gifts and talents fully. We need to surround ourselves with like-minded people who inspire, nurture and support us, while we give the same in return.

4. **Rejection works in your favor** – Rejection hurts and can bring out the worst in us, but it doesn't have to be this way. Rejection is a part of life. Its nature's weeding out process that clears our path to set us on the right journey.

5. **Be the architect of your life** – We are not doing ourselves or anyone else a favor by having the wrong people like us for saying "yes" when we want say "no".

6. **Meet challenges instead of avoiding them** – Take calculated risks and be willing to be uncomfortable in order to achieve your goals. Seeing yourself accomplishing tasks boosts your inner confidence.

7. **Empowered Thinking** - When understood and applied brings about positive change. Strive to make your situation better, making use of the power, skills, and resources that you have, as opposed to acting powerless in the face of a problem.

So You Want a Mentor?

"The delicate balance of mentoring someone is not creating them in your own image, but giving them the opportunity to create themselves."

Steven Spielberg

Questions for You:

What qualities do you seek in a mentor?

How can a mentor help you accomplish your goals?

What can you offer your potential mentor in return?

As a woman in business, no matter what your age or experience level, relationships are important. How you maintain those relationships is even more important. I can't stress that enough.

It's easy to see someone you deem as successful and want them to mentor you. This person appears to have success that you want to emulate. You want to know their secret and how you can be where they are. You want to pick their brain over lunch or coffee.

As the actor/comedian, Martin Lawrence, said in his standup film, Runteldat:

> "STOP, THINK ABOUT IT!"

Picking someone's brain isn't appealing. Just those words alone will turn someone off these days. Once upon a time, it may have worked, but now with anyone able to message executives through LinkedIn, Twitter, etc., people get hit with these offers several times a week. It's time to develop a new strategy.

Tips:

1. Before sending that email or approaching someone at an event, see if your potential mentor of choice is hosting their own event, a class or webinar that you can attend. This is a better way of "picking someone's brain."

    a. Why? – It shows that you support them and by attending you may actually get your questions answered and can save the time and effort it will take to try getting them to be your mentor.
    b. Why? – If you do decide to reach out to them, you'll have a point of reference. You can mention something they said that spoke to you and that can lead to a conversation.

2. A mentor-mentee relationship should not be all about you and what you want. Find something of value that you can offer your mentor, it can be as simple as suggesting a new restaurant or keeping them up on the latest trends.

3. Be clear about what it is you are looking for from your mentor. You must have topics on hand that you will like to discuss to save your time and that of your mentor.

4. There are different levels of mentoring – peer mentors are also great to learn from, so don't

be so focused on the people speaking at an event, the person next to you could also be of equal or greater value.

5. Join a professional association, social club, or meet up group to gain direct access to the type of people you want to meet.

6. Websites such as micromentor.org and score.org/mentors are setup exclusively just for establishing mentorships.

7. Be open-minded about your journey to finding the right mentor. Remember that good mentoring goes beyond offering good advice. It's a relationship that can change your life. A mentor will provide valuable time and effort to help you reach your goals.

> "Your true self-worth is up to you. Increase it. Don't allow your life's pursuit to be caught up in the acquisition of material things – that makes for a nice net-worth, but not necessarily a high self-worth. And self-worth trumps net-worth any day."
>
> - Joshua Becker

STARTUP GUIDE

READY. SET. GO

Grab a pen and notebook and let's lay the groundwork for starting your business!

This business startup guide -- if you answer all the questions honestly--will help you collect and evaluate essential information about yourself and the business you would like to start.

While it won't give you all the facts you need to determine if you should pursue your business idea, it will help you answer some very fundamental questions and help you identify possible pitfalls that most business owners encounter.

Women Owned Business in the United States

- More than 9.1 million firms are owned by women, employing nearly 7.9 million people, and generating $1.4 trillion in sales as of 2014.
- Women-owned firms (50% or more) account for 30% of all privately held firms and contribute 14% of employment and 11% of revenues.
- Over the past seven years, the overall increase of 8.3 million (net) new jobs is comprised of a 9.2 million increase in employment in large, publicly traded corporations, combined with a 893,000 decline in employment among smaller, privately held companies.

Businesses Owned by Women of Color

- 2.9 million firms are majority-owned by women of color in the U.S.
- These firms employ 1.4 million people and generate $226 billion in revenues annually.

Million Dollar Businesses

- One in five firms with revenue of $1 million or more is woman-owned.
- 4.2% of all women-owned firms have revenues of $1 million or more.

Source: National Association of Women Business Owners

BUSINESS START UP CHECK LIST

- Choose a business based on your level of skills and interests.
- Research the business idea
    - What will you sell?
    - Is it legal?
    - Who will buy it and how often?
    - Are you willing to do what it takes to sell the product?
    - What will it cost to produce, advertise, sell, and deliver?
    - With what laws will you have to comply?
    - Can you make a profit?
    - How long will it take to make a profit?
- WRITE A BUSINESS PLAN AND MARKETING PLAN
- Choose a business name
- Verify right to use the name
- See if the business name is available as a domain name
- Register the domain name if you aren't ready to use
- Set up an email address
- Set up social media accounts
- Register the business name and get a business certificate
- Choose a location for the business or make space in the house for it
- Check zoning laws
- File corporation papers

- Get any required business licenses or permits
- Register for a trademark
- Register copyrights
- Apply for a patent (if applicable)
- Open a bank account for the business
- Have business cards and flyers printed
- Purchase equipment and/or supplies
- Order inventory
- Order signage
- Get your website set up
- Get professional headshots of yourself
- Get professional photos of your products
- Have business literature prepared
- Let everyone know that you are in business

BUSINESS PLANNING GUIDE

COVER SHEET
STATEMENT OF PURPOSE
I. BUSINESS PLAN
    A. DESCRIPTION OF THE BUSINESS
    B. PRODUCT OR SERVICES
    C. MARKET
    D. MARKETING STRATEGY
    E. COMPETITION
    F. LOCATION
    G. PRODUCTION PLANS
    H. MANAGEMENT
    I. PERSONNEL
    J. APPLICATION AND EXPECTED EFFECT OF LOAN

II. FINANCIAL DATA
III. FINANCIAL PROPOSAL
IV. SUPPORTING DOCUMENTS

COVER SHEET:

Name of Business, Principals, Address, Business Phone, Business Email, Business Website

STATEMENT OF PURPOSE:

- Who is asking for money?
- What is the business structure? Explain ownership
- How much money is needed?
- How will the funds benefit the business?
- Why does the loan or investment make sense?
- How will the funds be repaid?

I.   BUSINESS PLAN

PART A. DESCRIPTION OF THE BUSINESS

1. History of the company, status (start-up, expansion, etc.)
2. Description of the business.
3. Why will the business work and be profitable?
4. How does it fit into the marketplace?
5. What will the future hold?

PART B. PRODUCT OR SERVICES

1. Give a complete description of what you plan to sell.
2. If possible, include a photograph, drawing, blueprint of the product(s).
3. Emphasize the basic product, which will be the bulk of income and profit margin.

4. Explain advantages, benefits, and anything about your products or services.

PART C. MARKET

1. What is the total universe of your market?
2. Is the industry growing or declining? At what rate?
3. Is anything happening or expected to happen in the future that will have an impact on your business? (Market's Potential Growth)
4. What is the present size of the market?
5. What percentage of the market will you have?
6. How are you going to satisfy your market (customers)?
7. How are you going to price your product, service, or merchandise to make a fair profit and at the same time, be competitive?
8. Who will your customers be?
9. Why will they buy your product or service?

PART D. MARKETING STRATEGY

1. Describe how your product or service will be sold.
2. How will you attract and keep this market?
3. How can you expand your market? By what time frame?
4. What price do you anticipate getting for your product?
5. How did you arrive at this price? Is it a profitable margin?
6. Is the price competitive?

7. Why will someone pay your price?
8. Describe your advertising and public relations plans, plus any service and warranties policies?
9. Include any marketing research completed for the business.

PART E. COMPETITION

1. Who are your four or five key competitors? Generally describe your competition.
   a. Geographically
   b. Most similar product line
2. How will your operation be better than your competitors?
3. How is your competitors' business – Steady? Increasing? Decreasing? Why?
4. How are your competitors' operations similar or dissimilar to your operations?
5. What are the strengths and weaknesses of your competitors?
6. What have you learned from your competitors?
7. If competition is weak, how will your business fill a need created by their weaknesses?

PART F. LOCATION

1. What is (will be) your business address? (If no address, ideal location)
2. What are the physical features of your location?
3. Is the building tailored to meet your specific needs?
4. Include a diagram of the building layout.

5. If renovations are needed, what are they? What is the expected cost?
6. Is the space leased or owned? State the terms of the agreement.
7. How do these expenses (rent/mortgage, renovations, improvements, etc.) affect your operating costs?
8. Why is this location desirable?
9. Does current zoning permit your kind of business?
10. Have you considered other areas?
11. What is the neighborhood like?
12. Discuss the traffic pattern. Will there be foot traffic? Is there adequate parking space? Is the location visible and accessible from the street?

PART G. PRODUCTION PLAN

1. How, where, and by whom will your product be produced?
2. What are the raw materials?
3. Are these materials readily available?
4. What is the manufacturing process?
5. What is the anticipated rate of production?
6. Will you have contact with the supplier to ensure a steady flow of materials/inventory and avoid a costly interruption of your business?

PART H. MANAGEMENT

1. Is the business operating as a sole proprietorship, partnership, or corporation?
2. Include a personal history of each principal.
   a. Business background
   b. Management experience
   c. Education – include formal and informal learning experiences which have a bearing on your technical, professional, and management abilities.
   d. Personal Data – current and previous address, special abilities and interests, reasons for going into your own business.
   e. Personal Financial Statement – only if the proposal is being presented for financing.
   f. Why will you be successful at this venture?

3. Related Work Experience
   a. Direct operational experience in this type of business.
   b. Managerial experience acquired elsewhere (past jobs, leadership positions in clubs or groups, etc.

4. Duties and Responsibilities
   a. Careful delineation of job responsibilities
   b. Organizational Chart
   c. How are final decisions made? Include decision makers and decision process.
   d. Major operating duties – personnel, production, sales.

5. Salaries (be reasonable)
6. Resources available to business
    a. Accountant
    b. Banker
    c. Lawyer
    d. Consultant
    e. Insurance agent
    f. Universities and Colleges
    g. Federal, State, and Local agencies

PART I. PERSONNEL

1. What are your personnel needs now? What will they be in the future?
2. What skills/qualifications must your personnel possess?
3. Are the people readily available?
4. Will you need full-time help? Part-time help? Independent contractors?
5. State the expected salary ranges and payroll details. Paid hourly, at what rate? Paid a fixed salary, within what range? Weekly or bi-weekly payroll?
6. Will overtime be necessary?
7. Will a training program be provided? What will it include?

*If you are running a one person operation, explain convincingly that you have the necessary skills and talent to achieve your goals.

PART J. APPLICATION AND EXPECTED EFFECT OF LOAN

1. How is the loan or investment to be spent? (working capital, equipment, inventory, and supplies)
2. Prepare an itemized allocation of funds – items to be purchased, unit price, number of units, total costs.

II. FINANCIAL DATA
- Sources of Uses of Funds
- Capital Equipment List
- Break-even Analysis
- Pro Forma Statements (if a start-up or existing business)
  Three year forecasts – Year 1 – monthly; Year 2 – quarterly; Year 3 – annually
    a. Income Statement
    b. Balance Sheet
    c. Cash Flow Analysis
    d. Profit Loss Analysis

Historical Records (if an existing business)

    a. Income Statement
    b. Balance Sheet
    c. Cash Flow Analysis
    d. Profit Loss Analysis
    e. Business Tax Returns

III. FINANCIAL PROPOSAL
- Detail how you will apply the funds (product development, inventories equipment, marketing, working capital, etc.)
- Input cost figures for each line item
- For Loans, explain the repayment schedule desired and refer the reader to the Cash Flow Analysis to demonstrate how the loan will be repaid with interest.

IV. SUPPORTING DOCUMENTS
- Resumes
- Credit Information
- Quotes/Estimates
- Letters of intent from prospective clients
- Letters of support from credible references
- Lease of Buy/Sell Agreements
- Legal Documents relevant to the business
- Census/Demographic Data

RESOURCES

START-UP ASSISTANCE

- **U.S. Small Business Administration**
  www.sba.gov

- **SCORE** - Free Small Business Counseling
  www.score.org

- **Small Business Development Centers**
  www.sba.gov/tools/local-assistance/sbdc

- **Business Plans**
  www.bplans.com

- **Expertise.com**
  www.expertise.com/small-business

CONTENT & CONNECTIONS

- **Women 2.0** - Offers content, community, and conferences for aspiring and current women innovators in technology.
  www.women2.com

- **Savor The Success** - Business Network for Women Entrepreneurs
  www.savorthesuccess.com

- **The BOSS Network** - Online Network for Professional Women of Color
  www.thebossnetwork.org

- **Networks for Women**
  www.networksforwomen.com

- **She Owns It -- Conference Listings**
  http://sheownsit.com/conferences-events/

- **Little Pink Book**
  www.littlepinkbook.com

- **Dell's Women Entrepreneur Network**
  http://www.dell.com/learn/us/en/uscorp1/women-powering-business?s=corp

THREE BOOKS I RECOMMEND

Required Reading for Business Owners

The E-Myth Revisited by Michael Gerber

Motivate Yourself

Choose Yourself! by James Altucher

The Magic of Thinking Big by David Schwartz

Be Inspired by Those that Came Before You

The Little Black Book of Success: Laws of Leadership for Black Women by Elaine Meryl Brown, Marsha Haygood, and Rhonda Joy McLean

More titles are listed under the Resource section on the #100BusinessGirls website. If you need any personal recommendations on what to read, please feel free to email me. Describe what you would like to learn more about and I can point you in the right direction. Yes, I do read and respond to my emails.

Connect with me at jamillah@100BusinessGirls.com

Connect with #100BusinessGirls

www.100BusinessGirls.com

Twitter: @100BusinessGrls – no "i" in girls

Facebook: Facebook.com/100businessgirls

Instagram: @100BusinessGirls

Email: info@100BusinessGirls.com

www.ingramcontent.com/pod-product-compliance
Lightning Source LLC
Chambersburg PA
CBHW051816170526

45167CB00005B/2036